H
SPEAK LIKE A
CAPE CODDER
An Old Salt's Dictionary

GEORGE B. HIGGINS

FOREWORD BY JOHN A. ULLMAN

EDITED BY GREG O'BRIEN

ILLUSTRATIONS BY GORDON BROOKS

CODFISH

PRESS

a division of Stony Brook Group
*"where the lobstermen speak only to oystermen,
and the oystermen speak only to cod..."*

In cooperation with:

Cape Cod, Massachusetts
www.oncapepublications.com

Published by Codfish Press
A division of the Stony Brook Group
25 Stony Hill Road
Brewster, Ma. 02631
Greg O'Brien, editor and president

ISBN: 0-9719547-9-8

Grateful acknowledgement is made for permission to
reprint cartoons from Gordon Brooks

Cover design, page layout and production by
Joe Gallante, Coy's Brook Studio, Harwich, MA

Special thanks to Elizabeth Shook of Brewster for her invaluable
editorial assistance on this project, and to Frank Guinan, Ray Artigue
and Mary Catherine O'Brien for their inspiration.

Printed in Canada

To the memory of my father:
George Henry Higgins

The greatness, the simplicity,
the humility, the pride,
the strength, and the goodness of Cape Cod
were all rooted deeply within him.

He had "sprawl"

Nam et ego filius fui patris mei...
Tenellus et unigenitus coram matre mea.
Proverbs 4:3

And
To Linville David Higgins
Filio Dilectissimo
1954-2002

"...et absterget Deus omnen lacriman ab oculis eorum,
et mors ultra non erit."
Revelation 21:4

Foreword

It was a lot of fun, but somebody had to do it. A book that preserves the way old Cape Codders thought and talked has long been overdue. Not overdone, just overdue.

George B. Higgins of Eastham, eleventh generation descendant of the original Higgins family who settled Nauset in 1644, has been assembling words and expressions unique to Cape Cod. At first, it was a sort of linguistic hobby. Then it became semi-serious research. And then came the urge to publish.

George Higgins found Codfish Press in Brewster as the publisher, and the deed was done.

Now it is possible to learn that from Sandwich down to the very end of Provincetown, there has never been a railroad station on Cape Cod. Not ever.

Reading this book, a great deal of confusion to the latecomers and off-Cape visitors gets ironed out. This is where readers learn, if they didn't know already, that Nauset Beach is something of a novelty. Until the Cape Cod National Seashore came into being, the coastline from Orleans to North Eastham was called, "The Backside." Look at it on a map, and you'll see why.

Looking at the map can be confusing, of course. This is why George Higgins explains that while you are looking up from the bottom of the map, you are "going down" from the Canal to Provincetown.

If this book were a mere glossary, it would have historical value.

It is not, however, just a listing. It is a listing with commentary, written with the authority and brashness of a true Cape Codder. George B. Higgins—a retired Congregational minister, an Annapolis and Williams alumnus—has his own points of view. A little weird, sometimes a little archaic, but his own.

For one thing, he used the alphabet as headings, and never (until I brought it to his attention) found a word for the letter "E."

But he did find a word for the letter "V."

Vum.

It's just possible that George Higgins—listing and explaining words peculiar to Cape Cod, and detailing expressions mostly indigenous—is more fun to read than the words and terms he so uniquely comments on in his salty dictionary style.

Research is too strong a term for his work. Higgins did, of course, organize his hobby after a while. On three-by-five file cards, in fact, or maybe larger, but file cards, anyway. And he did something else a good reader with a good ear had to do: he banned entries that were not either of Cape Cod or the Cape Cod origin of Nova Scotian words.

When he learned that our grandmother, Hattie Peebles Hatch, expressed ladylike astonishment by saying—"My stars and garters!" —he nodded, said he'd heard it, but rather suspected it was northeastern regional dialogue rather than Cape Coddish.

No such foreign inserts were to be tolerated.

At the risk of revealing a sidebar interest of mine, I have

to point out that this new book by George Higgins is a product of Codfish Press, a division of Stony Brook Group in Brewster.

Codfish Press is seeking out—and putting between the covers—all the original Cape Cod material it can find, and it has found a lot. It is the product of Greg O'Brien, who launched his own writing career 30 years ago as a cub reporter on The Cape Codder newspaper, and was brought up in Eastham himself.

The combination of Higgins and O'Brien, a fine Irish double play, has the clout to create Cape Cod as part of a world totally independent of America, cut off by an artificial water body called The Canal, and insulated from the rest of the nation by a language of its own. But even so, anyone who sticks his nose in *How To Speak Like A Cape Codder* will emerge both informed and amused.

John A. Ullman

Introduction

It is my hope that this book fulfills a genuine need. There have been massive changes in the fabric of Cape Cod, as more and more settle here without roots in our sandy soil. With the passing of an older generation steeped in the history, tradition and vernacular of Cape Cod, it is inevitable that a classic dialect and idiom is abruptly being lost.

As a casual hobby, I have recorded over the years some of the expressions native to this Narrow Land. It has been a pleasant labor, for my own roots run deep on this peninsula. Since the arrival of the Pilgrims, my father's family has lived on the Outer Cape. From like beginnings, my mother's family was similarly rooted here, until just before the War of the Revolution when the family was driven out of Chatham as Tories, taking refuge in what became the Cape Cod colony of Cape Sable Island, down in Nova Scotia. Family legend records that as they set off in open boats, the following couplet was tauntingly composed:

Ye Highlands of Chatham,
We bid you adieu;
As Lot came out of Sodom,
So we come out of you.

Thus remote and isolated from the rest of the world, many a Cape Cod phrase survived in Nova Scotia, even more resistant to change.

Here then is a simplified "dictionary" of Cape Cod expressions. I make no claim to inerrancy, nor that this listing is even remotely complete. What follows is simply the result of one man's search along serious lines—sifted with a dash of facetiousness and whimsy. If it is of any significant worth, true credit goes not to me, but to many a Cape Codder and Cape Sable Islander of a generation that has or will soon pass from the scene. I think of the late Phil Schwind—Eastham fisherman, author and long-time writer for The Cape Codder—whose column rejoiced under the heading: "It's a Phil Scwind That Blows No Good." I remember "Ossie Paul" Nickerson, Will Cahoon, "Doc" Brown, Dewey Nickerson, Uncle Victor, and yes, my contemporaries—John Ullman, Don Sparrow, Ken Collins, Jim Kenneway, Tom Fuller, and so many others. Mostly, I owe an incalculable debt to "Gramp" (Cap'n Dave Morrissey). These words were his native tongue.

Enormous gratitude is expressed for these glorious cartoons that have appeared over the years in The Cape Codder and were contributed by Gordon Brooks. I cannot adequately express my appreciation.

Credit is also due the defunct journal of the American Dialect Society, 1908-1917, which was consulted to confirm accuracy.

Sincere gratitude is due and here paid to those who have suggested additional Cape Cod terms that are incorporated in this second revised edition. Keep them coming, please. The dialect has come a long way, and yet in many ways remains the same, ever since that very heated and uncomfortable introduction on December 8, 1620 when my Pilgrim ancestors encountered my Indian ancestors on the First Encounter Beach in Eastham.

And finally, blessings to my wife, Lynn, three sons and twin daughters, five grandchildren and two great grandsons—potential 14th generation Cape Codders.

G.B.H.
Maushop Acre
Eastham, Massachusetts
July, 2003

Si ergo nesciero virtutem vocis, ero ei cui loquor,
barbarus: et qui loquitor, mihi barbarus.
I Corinthians 14:11

How To
Speak Like A
Cape Codder

An Old Salt's Dictionary

*"Could we have high tide at three next
Wednesday – we have guests coming?"*

A-B

*"This year let's call it 'Regional Cuisine'
and jack up the prices."*

A

aback
To be "aback" is to be at a standstill, to be dead in the water.

accommodation
A horse drawn public conveyance.

ah (how to pronounce)
The eighteenth letter of the English alphabet. Elsewhere pronounced "r," but down Cape, especially following an "a," it becomes "ah." Obviously then, "Harwich" is rendered "Hahwich" and "Barnstable" becomes "Bahnstable." If readers want to be confused, they should know there are purists who insist with justification that the Town of Harwich be pronounced "Hawich" with a very long "a."

alewife
A "herring," a term derived from the Indians, but if you want to start an interminable argument, the origin of this term is a fair place to begin. "Alewife" is also descriptive of a woman who keeps an alehouse, but there are not as many of these left around as there are herring. If it helps, his (or her) true name is pomolobus pseudoharengus—the fish, that is, not the bar mistress.

Ambrose
A reference to one Ambrose Snow, long late of Truro, who

froze off both his legs in the monumental cold of January 1806. The unwilling sacrifice of Mr. Snow gave rise to the still current expression on the extreme Outer Cape, "It ain't been this cold since Ambrose lost his legs!"

anchor dragging
This is not a manifestation of poor seamanship. It rather describes a business that developed around the process of grappling for lost anchors and other sorts of marine goodies that could be salvaged for a profit.

antique
Depending on where you purchase one of these, it may vary from an Avon shaving lotion bottle to a dung fork, from a Shirley Temple mug to a thunder jug, from a Nixon button to a firkin. (That's a wooden bucket.)

antique shop, also ye olde antique shoppee
An establishment for the sale of the above items, ranging from an old barn or chicken coop to the parlor of a sea captain's residence; a place of business where tourists are well advised to check the gold in their teeth prior to departing, especially true when a sign indicates the existence of a "shoppee."

appletree fleet
Old coasting vessels that plied along shore, a term originating as a means of describing ships that never got beyond sight of the orchards on the coast.

ayup

An affirmative reply, roughly the equivalent of "yes." It may even replace "I do" as a legal response in a marriage ceremony. It also conveys to trained ears, "I'm listening to you, but I may not agree with you." Down in Maine "AYUP" becomes "AYUH."

B

backen round

Wind when it hauls around to the left or against the sun.

backside

The eastern side of the Outer (or Lower) Cape, facing the Atlantic. The Outer Beach is found on the "backside" and, please, nowhere else.

bagnet

A bayonet. You won't hear this term anymore. Those who used it have all gone to their reward, and besides in an era of inter-continental ballistic missiles, who needs a bagnet, as this charming item was called on the Cape when the world was younger, and so was I.

banger

A term describing something uncommonly large.

bankn'

Almost any steep slope reaching down from upland, applying

even to the cliffs of the Cape's backside of the dune embankments facing bayside. On the mainland it usually applies to the front yard as it slopes to the street.

Banks

Used in the plural, this has nothing whatsoever to do with institutions of higher finance. "The Banks" is reference to either the Newfoundland Banks or the closer Georges Banks—the source of the Cape Cod fisherman's better catch. A "banker" may be the traditional individual who handles your money, but he could also catch your fish.

barge

A horse and hack (not buggy) that was employed to meet the trains and transport passengers to vacation hotels—and to school—as late as the 1930's. Surely this is a more appealing term than "school bus."

barking bass

A dogfish, sometimes derisively called a "bow-wow," whose barking sound often greets a fisherman.

bayberry

A wild bush—often referred elsewhere as a "wax myrtle" or "candleberry," or if you get technical, "myrica cerifera." The gray berries are gathered in the autumn and melted into a wax used to make an especially fragrant candle. If you try this as a family project, prepare yourselves for a double surprise. You'll need a helluva lot more berries than you planned on, and unless you find a cheap source of heat, your bill for the use of the electric stove will boggle the mind. Better still, go buy some at a gift shop.

bayside
Cape Cod, as it faces (obviously) Cape Cod Bay.

beach buggy
A vehicle capable of being driven on the beaches without getting stuck in the sand, a statement members of the United States Coast Guard might effectively dispute. Few machines are more capable of exciting stronger opinions, pro and con, as to whether they are a blessing or a curse. You decide, as an old-timer, my views are stuck in reverse.

beachcomber
See "mooncusser," a far more picturesque term. In common usage today a beachcomber is thought of as the tourist strolling the beach in search of odd bits of substance, but years ago such activity bordered on being a profession, dedicated to the acquisition and disposition of profitable flotsam and jetsam.

beach plum
Another wild bush that grows in blessed profusion on the Cape, uncommonly called prunus maritima. In late summer and early autumn it produces a red-to-purple or yellow fruit the size of a small cherry. The fruit is made into a tart jelly that you can purchase at any number of roadside stands, a

far easier undertaking than gathering the plums and making it yourself. The latter course is, however, surely the more enjoyable to the extent that it gets you out in the queen of all seasons of the Cape Cod year.

beached pig

A blackfish (see "puffin pig") washed ashore and, thereby, a windfall to the economy in the early days for those who found and initialed this treasure, especially with the oil retrieved from the head. All of this held true generations ago. Today such an arrival is but a sad curiosity.

beam sea

Very heavy water, no doubt arising through reference to the beam of the ship—that is, the extreme breadth of a vessel at its widest point. When a ship is in such position that on one side her beams approach a vertical position, you are out on a "beam sea," and you're close to being on your "beam ends," a point when and where your material resources have just about run out.

Biblefaces

An old reference to the inhabitants and citizens of Wellfleet, probably a reflection on their traditionally dour expression—perhaps more unkind to Holy Writ than to the "Wellfleetians," as now they delight with gentility so to name themselves.

black back

Winter flounder or lemon sole.

blues
This should not be confused with the classic music of New Orleans, nor with one's emotions before (or immediately following) a holiday. On Cape Cod the only "blues" are bluefish.

Blunts
Old quahaugs worn round by tidal scour.

bog boots
An ingenious evolution from the snowshoe. Bog boots were designed to be fitted to the hoofs of the horses that worked the hay in the salt marshes. Nine inch square flat pieces of wood were clamped to the hoofs to prevent (with varied degrees of success) the horses from sinking. Old-timers often speak of bog boots, but the only example I have ever seen is in the National Seashore Visitors' Center in Eastham.

bog house
Communal housing for the families who handled the annual autumnal picking of the cranberry crop.

borm of fish
A reference to a fishing boat, returning to port after a good trip with a full catch.

brash
Windy, flatulent. "Those beans do make me a mite brash for days!"

C-D

"I know it's your mother, Velma, but the feller insisited it was a ship's figure head and gave me fifty bucks."

C

cackler

A broken quahaug, also an empty scallop.

cal'late

To calculate, so Joseph C. Lincoln insists on nearly every page of his half a hundred volumes. It is roughly the equivalent of "reckon," although this writer has never heard the word thus pronounced. Actually, on one recent occasion he did hear an elderly native refer to an instrument for the performance of mathematical operations as a "cal'lator."

Canal

The only truly significant canal, it separates Cape Cod from what remains of the United States to the west. There are, to be sure, other canals, such as Panama, Suez, Erie, et cetera, but when prefaced by "The," it can apply to but one body of water —The Cape Cod Canal. It is crossed by a native Cape Codder going west only with the greatest reluctance and sacrifice. Such a trip seems designed for the purpose of the native's learning just how much The Cape means to him. This being the case, he or she drives over The Canal eastward with great relief.

Cape antelope

There's no sense in trying to fake this one or to hide my ignorance. I haven't the foggiest notion what a "Cape antelope" is, or indeed if such an expression has any authenticity. It may be like the unicorn and the bluebird, purely a myth. If you challenge this observation, let it be recorded that after years of faithful bird-watching, this observer has yet to see a bluebird, leading to the conclusion that such a bird really is at best a myth and at worst a hoax. If anyone can track down an accurate meaning of a "Cape Antelope," then bully! I give up!

Cape Cod

Originally this referred to Provincetown and the Province Lands. In time it gradually was stretched up (or down, depending on your false sense of direction) to include the Outer Cape (q.v.) and then the entire peninsula (but never, never going beyond The Canal, although many a Wareham merchant would like to have you think this was not so).

Cape Cod Black Dog

No! Don't go running to the American Kennel Club for this one. The Cape Cod Black Dog is less than purebred—partly Labrador retriever, a bit smaller, endowed with a more pointed nose, and usually with a splash of white on the chest. Cape Cod Black Dogs are exceptionally good natured, be assured there's always a litter at the dog pound possessed of the unique ability to sniff your shoes and lick your face at the same time. I owe writer Paul Kemprecos for that one.

Cape Cod cottage

The most duplicated, least understood, and most prostituted piece of Native American architecture. Occasionally found on Cape Cod soil (or sand), it is surrounded with roses climbing a picket fence, but surely found on every street in Spokane, Ashtabula, Texarkana, and Tallahassee.

Cape Cod eels

These "draft dodgers" are long thin bags filled with sand and placed at the bottom of doors and windows to deflect cold drafts. Elsewhere these eels may be termed "snakes."

Cape Cod lighter

A lump of porous material—fixed to a handle, soaked in kerosene—that is used to light a fire. Actually, you didn't need to buy this book to figure that out. Any other dictionary would tell you as much, and you might be more likely to believe it.

Cape Cod minister

The sculpin, arguably the ugliest and most useless of all fish, so named for its big mouth and homely appearance—and good only for burying. Hey, I can get away with writing that! I've been one for years—a minister, that is, not the fish!

Cape Cod porridge

Or "Nantucket porridge." This is the sort of fog so thick as to clog your lungs and stick to everything from your socks to your drawers to your cap.

Cape Cod scales

I absolutely give up on this native term in the Cape lexicon. Can anyone out there tell me what they are?

Cape Cod suitcase

A cardboard box tied up with a string. It makes a good traveling companion. In the words of my Aunt Alda, "Who would steal such luggage at the merry-go-round at Logan Airport?"

Cape Cod turkey

See the reference to "salt codfish," but before you do, consider that "Cape Cod turkey" is a name with far greater character. No less an expert than John Ullman, who wrote the forward to this book, insists that this creation is salt cod boiled and mashed together with boiled potatoes and flavored with fried salt pork-fat.

Cape Codder

1) A native (q.v.)
2) A resident, whose definition is unacceptable to number one
3) An individual who lives on Cape Cod seasonally
4) Any person who loves Cape Cod, after at least two visits and grasps the truth that all Americans are divided into two classes: those who are Cape Codders; and those who wish they were

Cape Coddia

The ever-expanding corpus of printed matter dealing with any portion of the total ethos of Cape Cod. By and large it is safe to say that "Cape Coddia" is printed matter (as per this volume) and not literature. The exceptions to this—that is, those who produced genuine literature—might begin and end with Henry David Thoreau, Henry Beston, Wyman Richardson, and (with a slight stretching of the imagination) Shebnah Rich of Truro.

Cape-ender

A general and inclusive reference to the inhabitants of the last two towns on the Outer Cape (or Lower Cape)—Provincetown and Truro. It is rarely used even in reference to a North Wellfleetian.

Cat or Cape Cat

Not one of the feline species, but rather a small craft common to Cape Waters since it was created by Andrew Crosby and his sons in Osterville at Crosby Boat Yard in the middle of the Nineteenth Century. It is distinctive for its square stern, broad beam, and a single mast close to the bow. It has neither of bowsprit nor jib, and is known for "coming about quick as a (you guessed it) cat."

cat bass

A small striped bass (see "stripers") large enough only for feeding the cat, but don't dare do it without checking the size—of the fish, that is, not the cat.

certain sure

Just plain "sure," but the addition of "certain" does make it more positive, doesn't it?

chaney

Among the older and mostly deceased Cape Codders (unless they are more than 125 years of age), the pronunciation accorded to "china," either the crockery or the nation.

"character"

To an off-Caper or tourist, most Cape Codders; to a Cape Codder, most off-Capers or tourists. "What a character...a piece of work!"

Charlie Noble

The flue from the galley stove. I know why it is thus named, but I won't tell, at least not here. Perhaps it is sufficient that you know what it is and not why, nor indeed who, the late Charles Noble was. If you have a problem here, check with the author or any old and true Cape Codder.

cherrystone

A junior sized quahaug, somewhere between a litteneck and a chowder quahaug. This is one instance in which the tourists reversed the order of things. It all began with the cherrystone being the smallest of the genus until the New Yorkers on ordering cherrystones insisted they wanted "the little ones." Confused? Sorry about that. So were the New Yorkers!

chopper

A large bluefish, completely unrelated to a helicopter or any part of a set of false teeth.

clabber

To the rest of the English speaking world, clabber, the noun, is curdled milk, and so too here on Cape Cod. Verbally speaking, however, it describes a weather condition such as,

"I'd be surprised if it don't clabber up afore noon and give us a good wettin." Such would usually be said when the sky was cobalt blue, but long experience knew that ominous clouds were just over the horizon.

clam

Please, please pay attention to this one! The word "clam" is only to be used to describe the so-called soft-shelled variety. It is never, *ever*, meant to identify the quahaug. (q.v.)

clam chowder

A chowder with clams (or quahaugs, in which case obviously it becomes a quahaug chowder). Other essential ingredients include onions, potatoes (very few), milk, heavy cream, butter—but NEVER, under any circumstances tomatoes or the general ingredients of a vegetable soup or minestrone which New Yorkers have the unspeakable effrontery to call clam chowder, Manhattan style. To get *that* you'll have to take I-95 South!

clam hoe

This is not the sort of hoe to be employed in the garden; indeed, it's not really a hoe at all. It is possessed of three or four narrow tines with a short handle not more than three or four feet in length, used to dig clams. To the uninitiated it can become an instrument of glorious torture, uniquely endowed with the power to break a back, or at least slip a disk.

clam tree

Contrary to popular rumor, clams do not generally grow on trees. Clam trees found on Cape Cod are usually pine saplings stuck in a harbor to delineate the channel. A good example can be found in Rock Harbor in Orleans.

Cod, as a noun

The King of Cape Cod Bay. In the Massachusetts Statehouse, where meets the Great and General Court of the Commonwealth, the cod is identified as "The Sacred Cod," an action that helps some of us to restore our faith in the legislative wing of a government which often sorely breeds despair. Cod has rightly been sacred to every Cape Codder for more than three and a half centuries. Cod was held sacred when the Swedes and the Dutch owned Delaware and when Georgia was only a prison colony.

cod, as a verb

To kid, to fool, to make fun of; for example, "You ain't been coddin' me, have you?" Whether cod in the form of a verb derives from the noun above—or is a mispronunciation of "kid"—can only be determined by one more brilliant than I.

codfish aristocracy

Originally a term applied to the Cape Codder who made a sudden killing for a successful codfish catch. In time, however, it came to apply to any family whose newly established wealth gave them to feel superior to their neighbors—and they showed it.

codfish heads
That which the old rhyme tells us Cape Cod boys used for winter entertainment viz.,

> Cape Cod boys,
> They have no sleds;
> They slide down dunes
> On codfish heads.

Codfish heads also made especially good eating and were to this writer's grandfather, Cap'n David Morrissey, the absolute ultimate of a gourmet treat. For the record, and to be politically correct:

> Cape Cod girls
> They have no combs
> They comb their hair
> With codfish bones.

codheads
Knee length boots. If you know why they are so called, we'd like to know. Traditionally they were made not of rubber but of oiled leather. It is not impossible that the resultant aroma accounted for the name. Codheads were made water-tight by periodically filling them with oil that soaked into the leather. Such a boot was warmer and more comfortable than rubber, although assuredly the feet retained something of the fragrance of their presence long after use.

coof
In Scotland a "coof" referred to any particularly dull and life-

less individual. On Nantucket the term was applied to any immigrant from Cape Cod, and in time it was used to describe any off-islander.

come up thick
What happens when fog rolls in.

conservation
But for the cause of conservation much of Cape Cod would resemble Blackpool, Coney Island, and Revere Beach strung out together. In all Cape Cod towns there is a Conservation Commission, and you might well remember its cause in your evening prayers. Aye, and in your will.

cooging
The term means "visiting," and I'll wager you never thought that was what you were doing on a Saturday afternoon.

cork stopples
"A load of cork stopples" describes a fishing boat returning empty. If it helps you any, a "stopple" is Middle English for a "stopper."

corn and beans
No, this is not Cape Cod succotash. Rather, in place of paper ballots it was customary for voters to cast one kernel of native corn in the ballot box to show approval of a candidate, and one bean for refusal. A heavy penalty was exacted on anyone who stuffed the box with more than one corn or

bean. One wonders if a particularly warm and wet election day might not, in effect, have produced an edible concoction. Perhaps we should so reform the current electoral process, which is significantly worse than succotash!

Corned herring
In the 1880s, before herring were smoked, but after they were removed from the salt brine, they were referred to as "corned herring," tasting nearly as good as the end product.

country visit
This is not just a neighborly "drop-in" unannounced. A country visit is a long planned stay; it lasts the better part of a full day, and absolutely includes a major meal—possibly extending several nights considering the distance between Wellfleet and Waquoit over dirt roads in a democrat wagon.

cow storm
Rain when unaccompanied by wind

culch
The trash and rubbish picked up when one rakes for quahaugs. It consists of quantities of mud, sand, seaweed, and the varied offal of the tourist, like bottle tops. "Culch" is also any material laid down on oyster grounds to provide a point of attachment for the spat. (q.v.) In time, the term referred to anything tossed as "culch for the circular file."

cutters
See "rundowns."

D

decline
To go "into a decline" is to enter a period of deteriorating health, probably in the old days a sign of the latter stages of "quick consumption"—a laymen's term for tuberculosis then.

Democrat
A member of America's minority party (in many Cape Cod towns, that is). Before the long reign of Franklin D., there was a time when certain families of this persuasion were permitted to reside on the Cape for the sole purpose of breeding postmasters to guarantee mail service during national Democratic administrations. There are quite a few more nowadays, and increasingly those who admit to this political label are accepted as a somewhat respectable part of the community.

depot
A railroad stop, but never a "station," Actually, who cares now? They're all gone.

dinner
The main meal of the day—but not in times past to be confused with what most of the rest of America refers to as supper. "Dinner" is eaten at noon at the hour most think of as

lunch. Breakfast on the Cape is what breakfast is elsewhere, and supper here coincides with supper in the rest of America—only in terms of time, not of content. Here on Cape Cod, mainland ways are now in the ascendancy, and dinner at noon seems only to occur as "Sunday dinner" and even then rarely.

dippin'

Any particularly thin individual, usually a woman, might be described by this phrase: "That Hannah, now she could do with a mite more dippin'," implying the need more girth, as with the making of a candle further immersion in the wax would add some much needed weight.

dobbies

Often referred to in Eastham as "sand dobbies," these elf-like, goblin-type insects can be found in the sand dunes when there is no horse at hand to ride. Ordinarily they prefer to make their homes in the horse's mane, or so local lore says.

dory plug

A muffin, or a dough biscuit, for its obvious likeness.

double house

Now we're going to start a Donnybrook Fair. A double house is not a duplex, as found in Greater Boston. What most assume to be the traditional Cape Cod House (which originally had two windows on one side of the door—and none on the other, thus making it a left-hand half house or a right-hand half house) is really a double house. It is possessed of two windows on both sides of a central door. Experts in the architectural field will insist the "double house" is really the "house," and that the aforementioned is the "half house." Obviously the first home the Cape Codder erected was the smaller variety, and you can be certain a Cape Codder didn't regard it as only half a house.

down by the head

What one is when bowed low by great age or infirmity—or when a ship is clearly doomed.

Down Cape

Let's talk about this seriously. The direction from the Canal to P'town is east, north, and down, even as one goes down from Boston to Maine and to Nova Scotia. (Hence the title of the celebrated State of Maine magazine titled "Down East.") The reasoning is sound when one remembers that these regions were initially approached not over land, but by ship, thus traveling downwind, according to sailing charts. We may now navigate by car, but we still go down from Sandwich to Yarmouth, to Orleans, to P'town. If that seems inconsistent with sound logic and current transportation, it doesn't bother us a bit. It has also been suggested that every place from Boston (The Athens of America) is "down," which is to say "below," "lower" or "beneath."

drail

So called on the Cape, a lure for bluefish, bright, shiny, with a rigid hook at the stern.

drawing water
This has nothing to do with a trip to the well. One who may appear to be a perfectly delightful fellow, but who seems to be a mite short on character or intelligence, can evoke such a comment as, "Abner, don't seem to draw much water." The term refers to the large vessel that makes long voyages and rides deeply in the water with the small dory in which one might go "scowbanging" (q.v.) about the harbor.

dreen
A shallow salt water channel; also a guzzle. In a verbal sense one might be called upon "to dreen a boat," which is, of course, to drain it, as by pulling the plug.

dreener
A lath crate with handle. Supposedly clams can be washed in it by dipping it in clear water, but, my friend, don't count on that. It is also in some circles a hod, measuring some 9" by 9" by 19" inside and holding two, twelve-quart buckets of shellfish—usually only used with clams and razors.

drozzle
To spill, as: "Child, you drozzled your milk all down your bib."

dry land sailor
The village miller. When the arms of the windmill were set to sails, you can imagine the derivation of the term.

dry no'theaster

In any season a "dry no'theaster" brings on the finest of weather, although the more pessimistic of Cape Codders will see it as a "weather breeder." Add, however, some moisture, and you will have quite a different kettle of fish.

dump

A dump out here is still a dump. The signs may call it a "sanitary landfill" or a "transfer station," but to us it's still a dump. As well as with the post office, it is the primary source of local information—and misinformation—as can be found anywhere.

dune buggy

An automobile of dubious parentage used to travel over the dunes as a means often of spreading litter where otherwise it would be difficult to find. A close relative to the "beach buggy" (q.v.), the source of no pride either. It is of use only to those who do not have the time or make the effort to fully appreciate the Cape's natural glory. The only way to do so is by foot.

dunfish

Salt cod.

Dutchman's britches

When a slight slip of blue broke through heavy storm clouds, it was invariably accompanied with the comment, "There's 'bout enough blue sky up there to mend a Dutchman's britches." Repeated questionings since childhood have never evoked a satisfactory definition as to the quantity of blue sky required to repair such an article of clothing. Uncle Victor, highliner on Cape Sable Island, did tell me it was "about the size of your Aunt Bessie's bloomers." That didn't help a lot then, nor does it now.

E-F

*"I don't know whether to go to town meetin'
or to stay home and fight with the wife!"*

E

Eastham

I found it! In answer to John Ullman's suggestion in his gracious introduction, an obvious "E" entry surfaced just before press time. Missing it would seem as impossible as nailing a lemon meringue pie to the ceiling. Is any proper name so brutally and constantly mispronounced as Eastham? To boast the most rudimentary familiarity with Cape Cod, never under any circumstance give yourself away with emphasis placed on the first syllable. This is EastHAM, not that which emerges as a sort of EAST-um. It's not as serious a faux pas as putting tomatoes in your clam chowder, but it will twitch a nerve, and you'll be known as one from the western territories out beyond the Hudson or even the Connecticut River Valley. This is not just an idle idiosyncrasy. The name came from the eastern section of the borough of Ham in London; hence EastHAM. In time past, ChatHAM was thus pronounced, but over there you can probably get away with mispronunciation nowadays.

F

fart in a mitten

To run around like a "fart in a mitten" is descriptive of the sort of frenzied rushing of a puppy or small child. It has to be the ultimate mismatch of words, the origin of which is absolutely shrouded in the mists of total obscurity. But mother, nonetheless, accused me of it.

feather white
The surface of the ocean when a heavy breeze whips it.

feetnin
I like this one! Footprints—a term that gives rise to such a delightful comment as, "I seen—or heard—his feetnin on the road." Come on, admit it. It takes something to hear a footprint.

fetch
A verb that adequately replaces the word "bring" or "carry." Followed, however, by "up with," it means to "come up with." So, for example, an occasional manifestation of mental brilliance is a matter of "fetching up with an idea."

Figawi
An annual yacht race held each spring from Hyannis to Nantucket and back. The term "Figawi" is surreptiously a euphemism rooted in the concluding line of a bit of doggerel:

When it's foggy and gray,
And they can't find their way,
All the sailors yell,
'Where the figawi?'

fish corn

This takes us back to Squanto and the Pilgrims whom he taught to place a dead fish around a kernel of corn to fertilize the planting. Frederick Freeman in his History of Cape Cod informs that in 1718 the practice was illegal as it applied to herring. That doesn't mean the practice died out; it meant a switch to a different species.

fire and water

This impossible mixture of the elements is descriptive of the nocturnal scene when phosphorescent patches appear on the water, the result of large schools of mackerel breaking the surface.

flakes

Flat tables on which the Cape-enders (q.v.) used to dry fish prior to refrigeration, not to be confused with individuals who are especially flighty, strange, or peculiar. This noun, however, may well have emerged out of the verb describing the moving of various structures (once a very common Cape Cod undertaking) in which a building was often "flaked," that is, cut into flat sections to be assembled at its later destination. Noun or verb, which came first? I don't know.

flared

Slightly deranged as: "The last few months, Obed's been kind of flared; not real crazy, but sort of peculiar actin'."

flatfish

Not too exact a term, but it usually refers to a small summer flounder.

flats

The mud flats of bayside beaches at low tide. To go clamming, or quahaugging, is to "hit the flats."

floaters

When cranberries were hand picked in the bogs, those that were missed were floated to the surface by "flowing" the bog—that is, by flooding it. These "floaters" were then scooped up, proof again of a Cape Cod frugality which affirms that one wants not if he wastes not.

fluke

Not a mistake, nor an error, but rather the summer flounder or plaice.

fog

Pronounced "faag," this is an invader from outer space, which on arrival assumes complete atmospheric control over all phases of existence. It is especially the ascendant factor in Chatham. Indeed, the Tory Chatamites who immigrated to the Cape Sable Island clearly must have loved their fog insofar as the fog in their new homeland generally managed to lift for half an hour about noon twice a week—in a good summer that is.

fumigate

A common response to the age-old query by the summer tourist as to just what we Cape Codders do after the disappearance of the vacationers and the onset of the rest of the year, usually sounding something akin to: "Waal, we just sit around and fumigate."

fungy

I confess to having no idea how this is spelled—fungy, fungi, fungee, funjy, funji, funjee? However it is spelled, it is another name for "grunt." (q.v.)

G-H

G

gaffer

As in Old English, so in the days of the famous Boston and Sandwich Glass Company, thus was a foreman called. It may not be a wise appellation to use for your foreman back at the plant today, for it is essentially a contemptuous contraction of "godfather."

gam

Not a woman's leg. When ships were at anchor, especially in a foreign port, occasions to visit and talk with other crews made for a "gam." When fishing on the Grand Banks, dory men often went from one ship to another for a gam, an experience that gave rise to the traditional welcome: "Come aboard and bring your dory." It is perhaps relevant that gam also refers to a school of whales.

George Hardin

A "George Hardin" is a rundown (q.v.) filled only with mud. The story of why that man's name was thus immortalized is too long for this dictionary and too uncomplimentary of Mr. Hardin.

gift shop

A term to describe an enormous variety of establishments in which one may purchase any number of useless items (including this book) to remind the buyer of the little bits of summer gaiety and happiness. Items available run the gamut from "giftee shoppee junkee" to the finer objects d'art.

Gilligan hitch

Any clumsy or insecure knot, doubtlessly a reference to some unfortunate chap rejoicing under the name of Gilligan, remembered solely for his contribution to the sum total of the world's awkwardness. It is reasonably certain that he was close to another Irishman, Murphy by name, who gave rise to "Murphy's Law."

grass

Not, please, marijuana. This is asparagus, and none ever was produced of a finer quality than on the plains of Eastham.

gravestones

A set of prominent upper front incisors. Big front teeth!

greasy

An adjective that describes a calm, slick, and smooth sea.

Great Beach

The Atlantic Beach running from Chatham down to Provincetown on the backside of the Cape. When you walk it, you'll experience its genuine greatness.

Great Rock

Even the Cape Cod National Seashore mistakenly calls this "Doane Rock," probably because it is located close by the original site of John Doane's Eastham home on the road to Coast Guard Beach. This massive boulder was carried onto the Eastham plains by the melting Ice Age conveyor belt. This writer remembers when he could stand atop this rock and see both Cape Cod Bay and the Atlantic Ocean, both now obscured by the Outer Cape's thick blanket of locust and oak trees.

Greenbacker

This term was long ago applied to residents of Orleans, an evident reference to the reality that the financial center of the Outer Cape was (and still is) Orleans. Local Bankers and merchants held their neighbors in financial thrall—greenbacks being a rough translation of the golden calf so venerated in the Book of Exodus.

greenhead

An omnipresent female fly (if you want to get technical, her happier name is tabanus costalis). The male is black, pointed, and doesn't bite. The female frequents the Cape from the high course tides in July to the same in August. Like the tourists, greenheads flee the Cape after Labor Day. The female is easily identified by her green head (obviously). But have no fear, you'll recognize her even if you are color blind. Her sublime joy is to bite on immediate contact. The pain stays with you for several itchy days. Hell hath no fury like the scorn of a greenhead.

grumble and go

These words mean nothing different on Cape Cod than any-where else in the English speaking world, save that the Cape Codder has refined the art of grumbling to fine scientific perfection. This is especially true of the native fisherman. In the days of the clipper ships, a sharp captain wanted Cape Codders on his crew. For all that they grumbled, they did their work, and did it well. A Cape Cod sailor, he grumbles and he goes on with his work.

grunt

A term used on Cape Cod and among her descendants who emigrated to Barrington and Cape Sable Island in Nova Scotia in the late Eighteenth Century. It refers to a nearly indescribable mash of hot blueberries on a dumpling—a raised dumpling, that is, not the flat slippery type common to the benighted folk from Pennsylvania southwards. The term is probably descriptive of the guttural sound of satis-faction emitted from the interior regions of one who is pleasantly filled with this ample and rewarding food. Perhaps if an unhappy man can be disgruntled, then a happy one could well be "gruntled."

gubbins

Pan drippings, and called this for reasons unknown to me.

gurry

The guts of a scallop or, perhaps, any fish. In the process of dressing the catch a man could discover that a nick on the hand had become a "gurry sore." It was common knowledge that gurry fed to a cat would make his ears drop off.

guzzle
A small stream.

H

Hairlegger
A reference to the people of Harwich, lost to our age and even to the venerable Fredrick Freeman—Cape Cod's quintessential historian. There is, however, a strong suspicion that the name is rooted in the poverty of some of the town's citizenry. Unable to afford new clothing, the men were inclined to wear their pants until they crept up to being "highwaters," sufficiently short so that when seated, the hitched up pants would show some hairy leg.

half house
A misnomer used to describe what was, and is in fact, a true and full original Cape Cod House—designed with a front door and two windows on one side, none on the other. A left-handed house has the door on the left. You should be able to guess the positioning of the door on a right-handed half house.

hanted

An old abandoned house was never "haunted," it was "hant-ed," as were old lighthouses. Proof of this centers on my grandfather telling me of a "hanted" lighthouse on Cape Sable Island where all sorts of strange noises could be heard after dark. "What do they sound like?" I eagerly asked. "Waal, it's sort of like somethin' soft knockin' on nawthin'."

harbor blues

Bluefish weighing from three quarters of a pound to two pounds, not necessarily caught in the harbor; also "summer blues."

harbormaster

The appointed official who controls the harbors of the various Cape towns, he is endowed with a lordship in spirit that is actual, but in fact is not so easily executed.

harness cask

A stored up barrel of pork.

haul

To pull, as an anchor, or a tooth, or a truck wagon; also the wind has been known to "haul" 'round to the east.

health eaters

A snide put-down from another period of the summer visitors whose joy it was and still is to bask in the sun on the beach, to carry home a glorious tan, and to boost the income of the dermatological profession.

hearty

East of The Canal this adjective becomes a noun, referring to meat. On the authority of Joe Lincoln, it is "meat victuals," so that to "eat hearty" is not to eat well, but to eat meat. In older times, meat was seldom a regular part of any Cape Cod diet.

heave

To throw, as an anchor, or a ball, or a stone, or, one might suppose, even "the bull."

heave and haul

To cast for stripers or bluefish from the beach with a handline, that is to say, not with a surf rod and reel.

henhussy

The man who is a "henhussy" or who "henhussies" about the house, more especially the kitchen, is one who is too much under a woman's feet and generally very much in his wife's way—a common failing today of the husband newly retired.

herring pan

Any pan used exclusively to roast herring and, therefore, useless for any other purpose. It is usually relegated to the wood shed.

hide away

An expression, roughly the equivalent of "pine away," used to depict one who is closing in on the point of near or actual death.

highliner

The top fisherman in the community and the acknowledged leader of the fleet. This is a position achieved in small part by good fortune and chiefly by sheer hard work.

historical society

In every Cape town worth its native salt there is an historical society dedicated to the preservation of a goodly heritage. Historical societies do far more than just burn incense to their departed ancestors; they hold up before us the greatness of "the quarry from which we were digged." On a rainy day include the museum-homes of these societies in your itinerary. You may well remember this long after your tan has faded, and you've forgotten endless days on the beach.

hit the flats

A phrase used by the clam digger to describe a march forth into mortal combat with the mighty clam on the bayside beaches at low tide. To some it bespeaks a full time vocation, to others a part time vacation, and to the latter most assuredly it bespeaks an uncomfortable back on the morrow.

hog-age

The awkward years of a pre-teen boy. They can carry well over into the 20s for the especially immature.

hog's back son-of-a-seacook

This is not the term of reproach you might suspect,

although it is difficult to imagine a more creative one. Consider its application carefully before you use it as a means of hurling an insult, for it is in fact nothing more dramatic than boiled salt codfish with pork scraps. One suspects there is many a Cape sailor who could improve on it— the term, that is, not the dish.

hog house

Communal housing for families that worked the annual autumnal picking of the cranberry crop.

Hog reeve

There was a time on Cape Cod when hogs and sheep were allowed to run wild. When the law ultimately forbade such freedom, hog reeves were appointed to round up the hogs and put 'em in the pound.

homegood

Here's a choice one. It means shore leave from Coast Guard duty (or furlough, if your legs are oriented to land). Could you come up with a better term?

hooker

No! This is not necessarily what you think. A "hooker" can also be a boat that has fallen on hard times, and is about ready for the knacker.

horse mackerel

The mighty tuna, whose size ought to give the name some

genuine meaning. The tuna was thus described in an era when its value was considered next to worthless and was sold for cat food.

housen

To some this is the plural form of "house," while to others (and this with greater authority) it is simply the singular. So it exists in the dialect of Cornwall, from which part of England hailed many of the early Cape settlers.

hum ya?

An authority older than I (and there are a few) records that the only proper response to this query is: "Not bad (q.v.); hum you?"

Hundred Day War

The season of the tourist. A sure sign it is over is the blessed disappearance of New York Yankee caps.

I-J-K

"Hello, weather bureau? – I want to report that my husband is out shovelling six inches of 'partly cloudy'."

I

Indian tavern

Up-Cape near Mashpee, the term is used in reference to a heap of sticks. The origin of these piles is obscure, although they probably signified a sacred agreement or covenant. Upon each occasion of passing, a stick was added to the pile. Perhaps there is in the "Indian tavern" something of the spirit and the ethos of the rock Cairns of the Scottish Highlands and Herbridean Islands. "Indian tavern" was also the term once used by one of the Freeman Hatches, born in Eastham, to identify his stack of poles for string beans that he grew in his backyard garden.

Irish pennant

A loose end of a rope dragged from the side or stern, and not an indication of a particularly trim form of seamanship, nor a particular compliment to the Irish race.

Isaac and Josh

Whoever the original Isaac and Joshua were, they sound like the legendary Lancashire soldier, Private Samuel Small—the phrase "Isaac and Josh" being descriptive of things being at loose ends, all fouled up, "snafued."

J

Jack White

That's a shirt tail, and when Jack White is out of jail, there's usually a hole in the seat of your britches.

Joseph's garden

This has no reference to the garden of Joseph of Arimathea; it is rather a dory filled with earth and flowers, so named after the Rev. Mr. Joseph Metcalf, pre-Revolutionary War pastor of the Congregational Church in Falmouth, whose boat was filled with uprooted roses after a heavy storm. It does seem to be a rather undignified use for a retired dory, but in all fairness there isn't much left to do with such a veteran but haul it ashore, use it as a planter, and remember the old minister.

just night

That period of the day when evening or twilight is giving way to dark.

K

King's Highway

King's Highway, formally called Old King's Highway, is the bucolic, winding stretch of heaven along the Cape's north shore that most call Route 6A. Old timers still call it the Old King's Highway, a reference to a time when English on the Cape was spoken in the Mother Tongue.

L-M

"None for me, dammit."

L

left turn

Making a left turn in a car means the same thing on Cape Cod as in the rest of the non-British Commonwealth of Nations, except here in the summer months when it is undertaken with infinite patience and comparable risk. Experienced drivers plan their day's travel to be executed with an absolute minimum of such turns. It always gets better after Labor Day.

liberry

This is not a fruit akin to the strawberry or the blackberry. Much to the chagrin of purists in the field of pronunciation, it is the only acceptable way to pronounce a building devoted to the housing of a collection of books.

Lincoln

Anywhere in America save the Cape this is the sixteenth president of the United States; down here it is nearly as often understood to refer to Joseph Lincoln. By his 50 or so novels and stories set on Cape Cod, Joseph C. Lincoln popularized Barnstable County for several generations of devoted readers. It is safe to say that had he not lived and written here, many of you would not be as possessed with such a collection of conceptions and misconceptions about Cape Cod today. His truths and untruths do go marching on, just like Patti Page's: "You're sure to fall in love with Old Cape Cod."

line storm

With all the talk now of named hurricanes from somewhere in Africa, we've lost sight of the simple but violent "line storms" that rake our area. They tend to blow north in the spring and south in the autumn, and they can do it with great power.

liquor

Yes, as elsewhere this refers to whisky, rum, gin, and its cousins, but is also describes the juice left over after the cooking of flesh or foul—the source of gravy. Come to think of it, I suspect it beats the taste of any package store gravy you've ever had, and it guarantees no hangover!

litter

The offal of slobbus americanus ubiquitus, singularly unwelcome everywhere, both the offal and the slobbus, and especially so here on Cape Cod which is far too narrow and fragile to accommodate the refuse left by the thoughtless native or tourist.

littleneck

A small quahaug; indeed the smallest legal quahaug. See "cherrystone," which it isn't.

littles

Do a thing piecemeal, and you do it "by littles."

lizards

Tourists—an obvious reference to the ubiquitous Izod shirts, as well as the lizard-like appearance of the evenly burned and peeling victims of too much sun.

long legger

A hip-length rubber gumboot.

long price

That which neither a Cape Codder nor a Cape Sable Islander will pay. Either may fall short of the haggling techniques in a Middle East bazaar, but neither will pay that "long price" if it can be avoided with a bit of haggling. Aunt Mabel summed it up succinctly: "You never pay the long price, not if by hagglin' you can help it!"

long-tail sugar

Molasses, and rather a good descriptive phrase, as it is stretched and hardened.

loom

So do they pronounce "loam" on Cape Cod—aye, and spell it also.

lot-fence

The fencing—by now largely rusted out—with which another generation or two or three enclosed their burial lots in the old graveyards. Somehow they managed to survive the appeals for scrap iron that were heard throughout the land during World War II.

Lower Cape
The forearm of Cape Cod, basically encompassing the area from Chatham down (north, that is!) to Provincetown; the region is also called the Outer Cape.

lunch box fish
A small striper (q.v.), small enough to fit in your lunch box, having been divested of head and tail. At this time a striper is of illegal size, if it is less than 34 inches from the snout to the fork of the tail. Lunch boxes didn't use to be that much larger than today; legality has gotten bigger. Phil Schwind was always troubled as to how you could measure any fish with its head and tail gone.

lunker
A large striped bass; indeed, any large fish.

M

mainland
The rest of the United States. It commences at The Canal and stretches to California. It should be obvious that Cape

Cod is now a man-made island. Long before the digging of The Canal, however, there was a sufficient sense of isolation on the Cape as to make the rest of the nation seem as if it were a different world, which it was, and which—thank God—it still is!

making fish

The process by which, before the efficiency of refrigeration, Cape-enders dried their fish on flat tables called "flakes." (q.v.)

market gunner

A man of another era who made his living by shooting ducks and other shore birds to be sold at (you guessed it) market. The term carried no connotation of poaching. It was a thoroughly respectable and honorable Cape Cod living until outlawed in 1918. Probably no group of men ever so upset the ornithological balance of Cape Cod.

ma'sh

The local pronunciation of "marsh," even as the third month of the year comes out "Ma'ch."

mate

As a verb this word describes service as second in command to a ship's captain. Be absolutely assured that there is no offbeat suggestion involved when a Cape Codder tells you that he "mated under Cap'n. Silas."

mauger

The exact equal to or clone of "meechin" (q.v.), although "mauger" appears to be more commonly used on Cape Sable Island, while meechin (see below) surfaces more often on Cape Cod. "Mauger" or "meechin," if you look it, you ain't well!

Maushop

The legendary local and usually benevolent Indian folk god. His size vastly exceeded that of Paul Bunyan, which as evidence consider that Martha's Vineyard and Nantucket were supposed to have been created by Maushop dumping sand out of his moccasins.

meechin

To look "meechin" is to give forth a pale and unhealthy appearance.

Mid-Cape

That section of the Cape that includes Barnstable, Yarmouth, Dennis, and sometimes Harwich and Brewster.

Mid-Cape Highway

An engineering monstrosity consisting of a macadam strip designed by idiots to funnel maximum number of automobiles at comparable speeds onto a minimal strip of land with the greatest number of potential hazards.

million

Would you believe, a melon? If you challenge this, consult

the quintessential authority, one Shebnah Rich and his book *Truro, Cape Cod or Landmarks and Seamarks*. If Rich said it, it's good enough for me, and he said it—on page 128.

mog
To "mog" is to move along slowly. It is usually applied to Cape Cod workmen, as, "I saw Eben moggin' along the road, 'bout as fast as a senile snail."

mooncusser
The mooncusser was one who cursed the bright light of the moon that complicated his luring ships to be wrecked on the outer bars by means of false lights, sometimes hung on the neck of a horse, thus simulating the movement of buoys. There is NO factual record of such activity ever occurring on the Cape, although it was common enough practice on the Cornish coast of England and on the North Carolina shores. The term is often used now to describe any beachcomber who collects anything of use after a wreck. Such work is referred to as "mooncussin" or sometimes as "moonin." If, however, you use that latter term in the company of those of a younger generation, believe it, they will give it a very different scene.

moon island
A privy, with clear and obvious reference to the half moon cut into the door.

mugup

This may be two words, but it surely comes out as one. On Cape Cod (and Nova Scotia's Cape Sable Island) a "mugup" is simply a cup of coffee, often associated with a "dory plug." (q.v.)

mummychubs

Saltwater minnows.

mung

Also known as angel hair, brown wool, and to Henry Thoreau, monkey hair. This is the thick and gloppy seaweed found at the ocean's edge that remains behind as the tide ebbs. It is a curse to fishermen, while to some it makes even the waters of Boston Harbor appear more inviting and, if long enough in the sun, smells about the same.

N-O

"Could they jump in your leaves?
They're from the city."

N

nail slick
The condition of a piece of wood weakened by repeated nailings or rot so that it will no longer hold a nail.

Nantucket sleigh ride
A whaleboat and her crew—when towed behind a harpooned whale—are said to be on such a ride. On this transit one was not likely to sing the joyful verses of Jingle Bells.

narrow gutted
Mean in a stingy way, as: "Old Shube is so narrow gutted he'd let his brother's wife go on the town."

Narrow Land
An affectionate and very accurate term of endearment for Cape Cod, an obvious reflection on its width.

native
One born on Cape Cod. In contrast to the unfortunate child who was brought here at the age of three weeks, remained for ninety-seven years, and never crossed The Canal again. It is an honor not to be taken lightly.

Nauset
The old name for the Town of Eastham, and at that time incorporating much of the Lower Cape. In early records,

such as the "Yarbage Book" (q.v.), it is often misspelled, as it was surely thus pronounced, "Norsit."

near

Stingy, tight, close, as in "Zack is the nearest man I know. I never saw him part with a nickel without a tear in his eye."

'n'en

A quite normal Cape Cod contraction for "and then." Thus it would be observed: "Last sat'day I went up to Dennis, 'n'en I stopped in to see Aunt Thurza." If you challenge me on this, just check out Phoebe Atwood Taylor's perennial sleuth, Asey Mayo.

net dragger

A Wellfleet fisherman, easily identified by a tiny fishing net tied to his trailer hitch, supposedly identifying the driver as a native Wellfleetian or more commonly known as "Fleetian."

New Comers

All other residents of Nauset who cannot be described as "Old Comers." (q.v.)

nigh

The exact equal to and replica of "near." (q.v.)

Nimshi

Something of a madman, especially when it comes to driving

a horse, a chariot, a wagon, or, one might assume, a fliver. Biblical scholarship failed the Cape Codders of another era (see II Kings 9:20), who assumed that Nimshi was guilty of the chariot racing of his son or his grandson, Jehu, depending on the interpretation. Whatever the case, there are still a lot of Nimshis driving about Cape Cod.

northeaster
Pronounced "no'theaster," not "nor'easter," this is a storm that sets in from the northeast (obviously!!); it is usually of several days duration, which, when it hauls in, controls all life from the time of its first prediction to a point at least two weeks after it has passed and the cleaning up is beginning to trail off. It is the sort of storm, as they say, that will "blow the stink clean off you." Significantly in the "Yarbage Book" north is actually spelled "no'th."

North Sea
Not the body of water off Scotland, which may be a bit of a shock to the oilmen who ply their trade there, but rather Cape Cod Bay as it appears to the Cape Codder of the Upper Cape.

north side of the oven
That part of the stove where items are places that need to be cooked slowly, close by the copper tank for hot water. Clearly, we're not talking about your new microwave oven.

northwester

A storm out of the northwest, although the "Yarbage Book" would have it as "west no'therly," which surely is a term unique to the Narrow Land.

not bad

A normal response to a casual greeting or inquiry as to the state of your health. The true Cape Codder is never "good" or "fine." He is "not bad," signifying anything in the spectrum that runs from absolute perfection to a near death experience when one expects to go under the grass so very soon.

O

off-Caper

One suffering the misfortune of not being born on Cape Cod, and one whose parents, grandparents, and great grandparents were not born here, either—a regrettable condition remedied only by a wise choice of ancestors.

oilskins

Foul weather gear that is sufficiently oiled to keep out the same. It is a far cry from your traditional raincoat, Burberry or London Fog, in appearance, weight, and aroma. It is worn with a "sou'wester." (q.v.)

Old Comers

A term used to describe the settlers who arrived at Plymouth
on the first three ships, namely the *Mayflower*, the *Fortune*,
and the *Anne*. Specifically on the Outer Cape, one of the
seven families of Pilgrims who rowed across Cape Cod Bay
in 1644 from Plymouth to Nauset, later Eastham, together
with present day Truro, Wellfleet, Orleans, and parts of
Chatham, Harwich and Brewster. They were: Thomas
Prence, Edwards Bangs, John Doane, Richard Higgins (I had
to get him in), Nicholas Snow, Josiah Cook, and John
Smalley. Actually the writer is descendant of all these
families save the latter, whose family was too small for him.
(Sorry about that). The term was used sometimes with
reference to their immediate descendants, who by now have
multiplied to nearly astronomical numbers.

Old Salt

Salt was used as a preservative before the refrigerator. On
long voyages, the salt would be piled high in heaps for six
months at a time. Today, the term "Old Salt" refers to a Cape
Codder (or a Cape Codder wannabe) who has seen his or her
share of changing tides.

old-timer

Any Cape Codder who has exceeded the age of eighty-five
has reached the point in life where they may commence to
qualify for this honor—a position he or she is likely to occu-
py for at least a decade. When one becomes the oldest resi-

dent in town, he or she is awarded the Boston Post Gold Headed Cane, although in some towns the cane is as much of the past as the defunct Boston Post.

on Cape Cod

You may well live in the Yucatan, in Cape May, in Katmandu, in Seattle, in Cape Ann, in Cape Hatteras; you may even visit in all these places. But you live *on* and visit *on* Cape Cod. The Cape is an island, manmade of course, but when you are here, you are not in Cape Cod, you are *on* Cape Cod. And being on Cape Cod is a blessing.

open up

that which the "flats" (q.v.) do when the tide recedes, allowing one to move in and dig clams. Actually, the tide allows you to do this twice daily, but if you're new at it, once is probably sufficient.

Outer Beach

That beach which stretches from Provincetown up to Chatham facing the Atlantic, also referred to as the Great Beach.

Outer Cape

The forearm of Cape Cod, it incorporates Chatham, Harwich, Brewster, Orleans, Eastham, Wellfleet, Truro, and Provincetown.

oyster

The vanishing native Cape Codder, alas. The oyster's lot on
the Cape has not been a happy one. For several centuries its
prosperity has risen and fallen. Sometimes native, often
transplanted from Long Island and the Chesapeake, when
the oyster is well and healthy, it is a delicacy unexcelled, but
woe the omnivorous virus.

P-Q

"– then if it rains let's have it at my place."

P

peak-ed

Note that this is pronounced with two syllables, the accent on the first. To "look peak-ed" is to appear drawn, thin, and emaciated, as, "Ev Snow sure looks peak-ed as a sick flounder."

piecen

To piece—especially to put together patchwork quilts, under which there is nothing more comfortable to sleep.

plum pudding voyage

New England whalers, whose voyages could reach two years and more, used this term to describe the shorter expeditions of many Provincetown whalers whose voyages were often of a shorter duration. The clear implication was that such were mild undertakings, all the while forgetting how often these ships from P'town were frozen into the Arctic and attacked by Pacific islanders, not to mention chased by Confederate ships during the War of the Rebellion.

pole

A fishing instrument, generally non-existent on the Cape. One finds here only a "rod," although the top-notch highliner (q.v.) may use the term "fishpole" when the pole is so much a part of his being as to be a veritable extension of his arm.

porgy
See "scup."

Portygee
A Cape Codder, as native now as any twelfth generation descendant of the English Pilgrims, of Portuguese and Cape Verdean extraction.

Portygee parliament
A meeting in which everyone talks and no one listens. This is often descriptive of town meetings. (q.v.)

Porty Reek long lick
Puerto Rican molasses. Think about it.

post holing
The art of digging for single razor clams; it is almost as hard on the back as digging a true post hole.

pottle
The measure of two quarts to a bushel, the share allotted to the village miller; it's really a pretty good deal, both for the farmer and the miller.

pox acre
The burial ground for victims of smallpox, a place singularly avoided by Cape Codders of another era. They wouldn't even go near to pick blueberries fifty years after the last burial.

pretty good
Not as good as "not bad" (q.v.). You figure it out, but be advised logic is not necessarily the key to unlock the mysteries of Cape Cod linguistics.

P'town
Provincetown, of course. Really now, some of these things you should figure out for yourself.

puckerstruck
To be "all puckerstruck" is to suffer the results of any especially disturbing experience. No doubt this is a reference that carries us all the way back to old "Puck," that mischievous goblin-type, sort-of-evil spirit of timeless lore.

puffin' pig
A porpoise; also a blackfish. When the latter washed ashore, it was a blessing to the finder who became thereby keeper of a first-class financial windfall. That was, however, in another age. Today such a find becomes a curse to be towed far enough out to sea as not to wash back, replete with an even stronger odor— or if it does, hopefully to arrive on the next town's beach.

puss (aye, and nuss, and wuss)
The archaic and dying (if not already expired) pronunciation of "purse," "nurse," and "worse." As with "sheer" and "chaney" (q.v.), these are hangovers of 350 years of duration (and that's some hangover!) from Cornish origins. So says Shebnah Rich, nor do I choose to challenge him.

Q

quahaug

There are off-Capers with the audacity and stupidity to call these cherrystones or little-necks—clams, a shocking error this, and unforgivable east of The Canal! The quahaug is the round or hardshelled member of the genus—venus mercenaria. For the benefit of those who have lost their Latin, that means "pretty money," surely a wise designation, for this was the shellfish used by the Indians for wampum. Incidentally, quahaugs you "rake," but clams you "dig." For many years Cape Codders have rightly been unwilling to put much trust in the dictionary, when it has the unwisdom to refer to the quahaug as a clam. Right now I have before me an otherwise very accurate and useful "Webster" that says under the heading of "quahaug"—"see clam." Any damned fool knows that if you look at a quahaug, you won't see a clam!!!

quaint

A vastly overworked adjective used to describe so many aspects of Cape Cod. Since the word basically means pleasingly suggestive of the customs and appearance of former generations, it is doubtlessly an accurate word. One wishes that those who publish the tourist brochures could find an alternative.

R-S

*"They're good, Beulah, but they're no match
for the Spring Peepers."*

R

racer

A codfish with a large head and a slim body, probably the result of some disease; any poor, thin, or spent fish.

rain

An atmospheric condition alluded to by Cape Cod brochures, carrying the strong implication that it almost never occurs here, nor does it disappear with the use of such euphemisms as "mist" or "low hanging cloud." Rain does fall on the Cape, however, and in the summer it is the joy of shop owners, who delight to behold the tourist off the beach and in their shops.

rat

A small striper, especially when the stripers are running large.

razor fish

True name on the Cape for the razor "clam."

Republican

Long the dominant political persuasion on Cape Cod for as far back as the memory of the oldest native's grandfather can recall, but the times are changing.

retirement

The goal of so many who visit Cape Cod and look forward to the day when they can cross The Canal and live on the "Narrow Land." (q.v.) Once thus settled, the retired citizen usually takes on more jobs and works harder, longer hours than the native, or than he did back in real life.

rootle

Cape pigs don't root, they rootle.

Route 6

A double-lane, narrowing to a single-lane highway stretching from the Sagamore Bridge to P'town, designed to carry tourists onto the Cape and dump them square in the Atlantic Ocean off Race Point. It is a stretch of road impossible to cross or to navigate with real safety from Decoration Day to Labor Day without infinite caution. The other nine and a half months it is an unnecessarily wide stretch of macadam, for all intents and purposes empty. By the time you read these words, alas, the ever-widening highway may be routed all the way down Cape to the glee of highway engineers, who, like the prophets of old, delight to drop their dynamite and run. Note that in Eastham, Route 6 was in better days called the "G.A.R." (Grand Army of the Republic) Highway, and so this writer still stubbornly names it. It should be noted that the G.A.R Highway springs up in Provincetown and runs 3,716 miles to Los Angeles, although it does get a bit obscure somewhere in Nevada.

Route 6A

An occasion to escape from the above, usually a delightful blessing.

Route 28

A highway of utter chaos confounded with confusion—from its clutter of buildings, to its muddle of traffic, to its misdirected directional signs put up by the state—north is really south, and south is really north. But no one up at the State House seems to care. They're all directionally dyslexic, preoccupied—we suppose—with the politics of the day.

rundowns

Large soft-shelled clams, five or six inches in length. They are best used in chowder. You don't hardly find them no more. John Ullman reports his grandfather called them "guilfords," and so did my grandfather. John doesn't know why. Neither do I.

S

St. Cedric's stone

A doughnut-like stone, with a whole in the center (of course). When suspended over a horse's head, it will free the horse from the power of the wee sand dobbies (which is thought to be a good thing—the freeing, that is, not the dobbies). It is supposed to be the source of good luck to any finder.

salt codfish
See "Cape Cod turkey."

salt mill
An ancient term for windmills used to pump ocean water into the salt works.

salt works
An ingenious arrangement for extracting salt from sea water by evaporation. It was a major element in the Nineteenth Century economy of the Cape.

Sandwich glass
Correctly used, the term refers to glass that emerged from the Old Boston and Sandwich Glass Company in Sandwich, one of the earliest glassworks in the country. Don't mistake genuine Sandwich glass sold at an antique shop from glass that was driven through Sandwich along Route 6 on its way from Japan.

scalawag
To some of you this word may point you towards a white southern Republican of Reconstruction days. In truth it is a sculpin, and some Unreconstructed Rebels may question whether there is any difference.

schoolies
Little stripers (striped bass, that is) from three to ten pounds in weight.

'Sconset dory

A cleverly and efficiently devised beach cart or wagon with a barrel for wheels, thus preventing this seemingly ungainly vehicle from getting stuck in the sand.

scowbanging

Wandering about without plan or direction, as in harbor a boat may wander from scow to scow waiting to be off-loaded enabling the crew to catch up on gossip in the same manner as their wives go "scowbanging" down Main Street.

Scrabbletowners

Natives of Scrabbletown, as natives of Chatham and especially its backside were called at earlier times in their very foggy history. No less an authority than Joshua Atkins Nickerson II suggests that it may be a corruption of "scramble," which is precisely what the natives did as they scrambled to launch their boats in the quest to board a stranded vessel and appropriate whatever could be seized. In the days of the "mooncusser," (q.v.) Chatham possessed not the best of reputations for hospitality to the shipwrecked. Indeed, tradition has it that one sailor struggled ashore and, on discovering he was in Chatham, jumped back into the surf.

scratcher

A rake with many long tines used to "scratch" for clams.

screening

In earlier days of cranberry harvesting to "go screening" was to serve as the final sorter of the harvest. The pay may not have been great, but those few short days of employment in the autumn could well make the difference that put a family's ledger in the black by year's end.

scrod

Be very sure and certain that scrod on the menu is not necessarily baby cod! In the classic sense scrod was whatever the head chef of the Parker House (in Boston, of course) named it to be—that is, the best catch of the day at the Boston Pier. It might be cod; just as well it might be haddock, pollock, or hake. Whatever its genus, enjoy!! Aye, and be impressed with another instance of Yankee frugality—calling just about every white fish "scrod" made changing the daily menu unnecessary.

scup

See "porgy."(Gotcha!)

sea clams

Sometimes known as sea hens, hen clams, surf clams, bar clams, and skimmers, these are found nearly two miles from shore; big ones best to be gotten at full high tide. These you use in sea clam pie, probably nowhere else. The authority for this is the late Cap'n Phil Schwind, whose word was always beyond dispute and final.

seashore

The Cape Cod National Seashore, a United States National

Park, established in 1961 and incorporating some 27,000 acres in Orleans, Eastham, Wellfleet, Truro, and Provincetown. This was a creative venture greeted with fear, mistrust, and suspicion at the beginning, but now recognized as the salvation of the Lower Cape from the ravages of the south shore of the Upper Cape.

season

"The season" is that period corresponding with school and summer holidays when the tourists arrive. It is a time of clogged highways, crowded beaches, busy shops, jammed restaurants, nervous cash registers, and weary year-round residents. It is a world vastly different from the other nine months. A good season carries the local merchant through the next nine months, probably as well as the profits of a three year voyage on a whaling vessel carried his great grandfather—and with considerably greater ease. Of recent years there have been efforts to stretch "the season" into October and back into May. Success is guaranteed as soon as the "off-Capers" realize the sort of weather available to them.

sedge clams

Small tender clams growing in the sedge grass found at the edge of a marsh or swamp. Sedge clams are designed to be steamed or fried. But watch out! They better not fall below legal size, which is two inches in length, and you'd better not dig in the sedge—not any more! Take note that "sedge" is pronounced "sage."

Seedcorners
A reference to a group of Truro whalers because their town of origin was the site of the Pilgrims' theft (or was it borrowing?) of the Indian seed corn; hence, any native of Truro.

selectman
The ultimate authority in each Cape Cod town. There are three or five of them, one or two elected annually to serve a term of three years. It is the highest honor bestowed by the electorate upon the citizen who covets being the most cussed at person in the community.

shade
"To have a shade on" in certain Cape Cod circles is, in a word, to be intoxicated, but short of the level of being totally out of the picture.

sharpie
No, not a slick and slippery card sharp, but a small craft about twenty feet in length, sharp and pointed both in bow and stern, nowhere near as maneuverable as that which largely replaced it, the "Cape Cat." (q.v.)

shearer
This name was applied to the furnace tenders, who, when they stoked the fires of the Boston and Sandwich Glass Company, were said to "shear the fire."

sheer

Share, as "half a sheer of," thought, by many, again, to reflect the old Cornish speech patterns transplanted to Cape Cod. In the old "Yarbage Book" (q.v.) of Eastham there is reference to a "sheer and pert," i.e., a share and a part.

shellfish constable

The authority indigenous to each Cape town on all things pertaining to the care, feeding, and harvesting of shellfish. It is an authority you'd jolly well better believe is an authority, if, for example, you end up with more than a ten quart pail of clams—or, indeed, if you confuse a quahaug with a clam.

sink box

A box, approximately three feet-by-three or four feet, set in a marsh on which to sit when gunning.

skimmer

One of several definitions for a sea clam.

skinch

To cheat, either in cards or quahaugs.

Skully Jo

A most improbable creation made from haddock. The fish was gutted, decapitated, cured in brine or salted, and dried in the wind. It was far better adapted to the driving of shingle nails or even for the foundation of a large barn. Chewed as a sort of "all day sucker," Skully Jo (aka petrified fish) miraculously seemed never to shrink no matter how long it was chewed over. The last recorded manufacturer down in P'town, one Cap'n. Elisha Smith Newcomb, succumbed in 1933, so that Skully Jo passed from the scene with the death of Prohibition. Make of that coincidence whatever you will.

Skurry Jack
A P'town fish salesperson. How's that for being politically correct?

slatch
A term used by the men of the Life Saving Service with reference to the slack water that follows the three waves which come in succession. The slatch is in turn followed by a backwash towards the sea and provides the best circumstances for launching a life saving craft on its mission of rescue.

slobber chops
A messy child, dog, or calf who spills food.

slough hole
An open area in a salt marsh, perhaps 12 or 15 feet across, generally good for quahauging.

slur
Variously used to describe the masses of collected ice that set into Cape Cod Bay, and, increasingly, a reference to any trash which polluting America piles up in Cape waters. With regards to the former definition, if you're sufficiently fortu-

nate to be on Cape in the winter, KEEP OFF THE SLUR!!
The children may think it looks like a great sport to climb
on and over. It is infinitely dangerous. One can so easily fall
through and drown.

smart

To look "smart" or to feel "smart" has on Cape Cod nothing
necessarily to do with one's mental acumen or one's high
style in clothing. Here and on Cape Sable Island this is a
commentary on one's health and vigor, so that a typical
greeting might well be, "Ain't you smart today?" To look
smart can also mean to be alert.

smurr

A verb descriptive of conditions indicating an approach of
heavy weather; hence: "It's smurrin' up for a storm." How
you determine authoritatively that it is, in fact, "smurrin' up"
is a matter of inbred insight.

smurry

A yellow eyed sou'wester—a hazy breeze from the southwest.

snapper blues

Small bluefish, five to six inches in length, and a great sport
for a fly rod. I know!

sneak boat

A bird-hunting vessel, usually of two configurations—one

with a kayak-like hull, the other with a "pumpkin seed" bow, quite wide and more stable. In both cases, the gunner laid back, sculling with one oar, leaving a low silhouette as to "sneak up" on the targeted birds.

snow

That which never falls on Cape Cod, and when it does, never lasts a day. For generations, we Cape Codders have been successful in affirming this truth, both to the world as well as ourselves. Having just dug out from a record winter of white stuff that never falls on Cape Cod, there could be something implausible here.

sober light

"The gray hour after sunset," according to no less an authority than Elizabeth Reynard. Perhaps our ancestors appreciated the need for special sobriety as darkness closed in and was not to be dispersed by the simple flick of a light switch.

southeaster

Would you believe, a storm out of the southeast? It is not correctly known on the Cape as a "sou'easter." Our speech patterns are sufficiently relaxed that we know we can do our own thing, even if it is more complicated. The emphasis is on the "th."

South Sea

The waters south of the Upper Cape.

South Shore
Cape Cod, as she faces south towards Martha's Vineyard and
Nantucket.

sou'wester
The weather when it is controlled by the wind out of the
southwest. This time the "th" is not used, so that it is never
a "southwester." I don't know why, and you don't really care.
It's also the term used to describe an oiled hat with a short
brim and a long neck to be worn with "oil skins." (q.v.)

spat
The young of the oyster primarily, but also of the quahaug or
soft shell clam, but never (I think?) of the scallop.

spleeny
He who acts "spleeny" goes about with a chip on his shoul-
der, an understandable term when one realizes that in days
past the spleen was thought of as the seat of the emotions,
especially the more melancholy ones.

sposen
Supposing, as: "Sposen we ought to head for harbor 'fore the
tide turns."

sprawl
Gumption; guts; ambition; "git up and git" will do. It's really
a fine and grand mixture of initiative, enterprise, and very
importantly contentment. It's that latter element that adds

the something extra to the lifestyle of the true Cape Codder. "They got sprawl!"

squawk
Or "quawk." This is the black-crowned night heron, not the great blue. Listen to one, and you'll know why. For good reason it is also called a "shite-puke."

squidhound
A big striper, again dating back to Shebnah Rich.

steamers
Soft shelled clams, used for steaming; their taste, once steamed, vastly exceeds their external appearance. They are also recognized as long-necked clams and are familiarly called piss clams for reason that is obvious, if somewhat less than elegant.

stifle
As in "eel stifle," a Cape Cod dish that tastes much better than it sounds.

stripers
Striped bass, or, if you prefer, roccus saxatilis.

summer beach
This is the elongated beach, possessed of upper and lower levels, the result of the gentler winds and waves of the summer season.

summer people
The true Cape Cod characters—the tourists whose arrival in the spring is a harbinger to local business that if they can endure to Labor Day, there will be enough in the till to see him through to the next year's invasion.

sumpy
Something I've never tasted, made from ground corn. You won't find it on the menu at the Land Ho! in Orleans, and I can't locate a recipe.

suncoming
Sunrise on the Cape.

sunsqaulls
Sunfish.

surfing
The art of riding a board in and over the surf. To those who are enslaved to the sport, it incorporates the ultimate in cold wet living.

swamp seed
Rice.

swept hold
A ship's hold, swept clean after the unloading of her cargo. "Swept hold" later became a common expression for a sailor's stomach when he was hungry.

swoll

The past tense of the verb "swell," so that if a skiff were kept submerged, the wood would be "swoll" and thereby tight.

T-U

"Could we have a side order of Quahaug Chowder with the Mai Goo Gai Pan?"

T

The Cape
A term used to identify Cape Ann, Cape Henlopen, Cape Charles, Cape Canaveral, but truly appropriate only to Cape Cod. It originally referred to the head of the land at Provincetown. In time "The Cape" inched up to Chatham, then came to include the entire isthmus. Chambers of Commerce just west of the Canal would like to believe that they are on The Cape. But don't let them get away with it!!

Thoreau
Henry David, of course. His classic book, Cape Cod, was descriptive of his walking tour in the Mid-Nineteenth Century. Just remember down here the name is pronounced as "Thura." It was then, and still is by a diminishing number of those who remember.

three quarter house
A Cape Cod "half house," (q.v.) to which has been added one window on one side of the door, in contrast to the original two windows on the other side. In essence it is a house and a half.

tie tags
To "tie tags" is to participate in a Nineteenth Century home industry in which women managed to earn considerable pin money (a rarity then, both the pins and the money) by tying string on sales tags. This was a time of tightened economy

and proved to many a family to be life-saving financial assistance.

tinker mackerel

This variety, Dewey Nickerson insists, isn't fresh if the tails have stopped wagging. It is the small Boston mackerel (scomber scombrus), running about three-quarters of a pound. They are also known as tacks, spikes, tinkers, and number ones.

toad grunter

Sculpin.

tongs

Long trousers, thus termed because of their likeness to a two-armed instrument of the same name. If you question this, just check the dress code from Enoch Pratt's *1844 A Comprehensive History Ecclesiastical and Civil, of Eastham, Wellfleet and Orleans* on page 178.

tourist

A paying guest of Cape Cod, whose coming in June brings joy to the hearts and cash registers of the Cape business community—and whose going in September brings even greater joy to the same hearts, but sorrow to the same cash boxes. There are those Cape Codders who would prefer these creatures to come as far east as Bourne and then just leave their money on one of the Canal bridges—and go quietly home.

town meeting

The ultimate in final authority in each of the town republics of the Cape. It is an occasion when the citizens assemble annually to direct town affairs, elect officials whom they will severely criticize all year, and raise and appropriate the funds about which their grumbling will never cease.

towner

An ancient Indian word of dubious origin, cried to signal that a whale has been sighted twice. It originated among the whale men when they were engaged in shore whaling.

traps

Not just a device to catch lobsters, traps also refer to personal luggage that was hauled around the world on a two-year whaling voyage or a three-day "country visit." (q.v.)

Truro grass

Not a form of Outer Cape marijuana. This is Truro asparagus. No finer was ever raised anywhere in the world other than in Eastham several generations ago. (Sorry about that, Truro). You can still stumble on wild evidence of this once major source of Cape income.

U

up back

Not to be confused with the Australian bush or outback, this is the area inland from Provincetown's immediate harbor area.

Up Cape

The direction back towards the mainland, where the advanced ways of Western Civilization and its attendant confusion drive men "Down Cape" (q.v.) towards Provincetown.

Upper Cape

That section of the Cape from the Canal including Falmouth, Sandwich and Mashpee.

V-W

"Could he call you back — he's working on his boat."

V

vum

To "vum" is to vow. A bedrock of residual Puritanism had many a Cape Codder somewhat loathe to make oaths and take vows. It was a bit more comfortable to say, "Well, I vum," rather that "I vow" or "I swear." Thus it would be that, when with excitement the young lad might rush up to Great Uncle Luther showing him a bucket of steamers, the response elicited might be "Waal now, I do vum"—carrying with it a note of wonder.

W

washashore

Anyone not born on and truly native to Cape Cod who immigrates to our sandy shore and makes his or her home here—a name justly appropriate to the Fulcher family whose ancestor literally did wash up on the Outer Cape generations ago, a survivor of one of the Cape's numerous shipwrecks.

weather breeder

Any beautiful day, as when the sun shines, the breeze is fresh, the sky is cobalt blue, and it seems too ideal for a true Yankee conscience to enjoy. Such conditions are sufficient to cause an authentic Cape Codder to denigrate atmospheric perfection with an "Ayup, it's not a bad day, but it could be a weather breeder," indicative of an upcoming period of sharply contrasting weather. Come to think of it, of course, every good day does breed contrasting weather—eventually.

weir
A fish trap or pound net, set in the Bay for the taking of fish.

Well, I wanta know
John Ullman, who wrote the foreword, reminded me of this expression of mild wonderment uttered upon hearing of a modestly significant accomplishment—such as managing to get the old flivver up a steep grade without the old machine stalling out.

Whiskin' fit
A seizure of frantic proportions that overtakes a Cape Cod housewife turning her into a housecleaning demon. She is only finally exorcised when the entire house is cleaned and scrubbed and polished from attic to cellar. There are reports that some were so victimized by the malady that they carried their efforts even to their husband's boathouse and woodshed—to no great welcome.

white horse tumbling over the taffrail
Authority decrees this to be a white horse (wave) coming in over the taffrail (upper stern) while the ship is running before the wind.

white water
The ocean whipped to a fury, having no reference to Arkansas which possesses no ocean.

winter
That time of year about which tourists wonder what Cape Codders do with themselves. It is the season when the native enjoys the peace and the fury of Cape Cod winter solitude.

winter beach
A more narrow beach caused by the erosion of winter storms; the sand is re-deposited in late spring by summer currents that build up the beach once again.

wracker
One who makes an honest living picking up the flotsam that is beached after a shipwreck. It probably commenced as "wrecker."

Y-Z

*"I couldn't describe my property, so
I brought some of it in to show you."*

Y

yarbage

The oldest spelling of this unique word is "erbage." It is the result probably of a local pronunciation of "herbiage," a reference to rights deeded for the cutting of marsh hay. The "Yarbage Book" of Eastham is a local treasure of no mean proportion.

Yellowbellies

A name bestowed upon Easthammers in the nineteenth century when citizens of Orleans were known as "Greenbackers" (q.v.). Yellowbelly was the common name for flounder or lemon sole. This probably afforded the opportunity to mock the courage of the Eastham fisherman. It gave rise to the delightful jingle, no doubt of Orleans origin:

> Eastham yellowbelly
> Can you swim?
> Yes, by God,
> When the tide comes in.

youmes and wemes

"You" and "we." A real beauty, these. Try them on your friends.

you sons'a'bitches

I'm sorry about this one, but it's significant, even if personal.
Grandfather never forgot that his Nickerson antecedents
were run out of Chatham as Tories. To my delight, he
(a good Baptist), instructed me that whenever we crossed
the town line into Chatham, we were to thumb our noses
and say, "you sons'a'bitches, we're back!" My grandchildren
today are as thrilled as once I was to use vulgarity acceptably.

Z

Zinjanthropus

A manlike primate of the Pleistocene epoch whose remains
were discovered in Tanganyika in 1954. Yes, I know, this has
absolutely nothing whatsoever to do with Cape Cod. I did,
however, note this to be a dictionary designed to carry you
from A-to-Z. I toss in, therefore, the best entry I can locate
under the 26th letter of the alphabet, as my contribution to
your serendipitous edification. Enjoy!

Nunc cognosco ex parte: tunc autem cognoscam sicut et cognitus sum.

I Corinthians 13:12

About the Contributors:

John A. Ullman, who wrote the foreword, was managing editor of *The Cape Codder*, an award-winning weekly newspaper in Orleans on Cape Cod. The author of three books, Mr. Ullman during his newspaper career was considered one of the finest columnists and editorial writers in New England.

Gordon W. Brooks, who contributed the illustrations, has been an editorial cartoonist for *The Cape Codder* for 40 years under the title, *Brooks Looks*. His cartoons have been published in more than 26 books and magazines. The author of two books of his collected works, Mr. Brooks operates a gallery called Brooks Studio on Route 6A in Brewster on the Cape, and is a professional violinist and cornetist. Since 1984, he has led a Dixieland band called The Clamshack Serenaders.

Greg O'Brien is editor and president of Codfish Press, a division of Stony Brook Group—a publishing and political/communications strategy company based in Brewster. O'Brien is editor and author of several books about Cape Cod and the Islands, a political columnist, a television and video script writer, and a producer of several documentaries.